EVOLVE
YOUR MIND

EVOLVE YOUR MIND

**HOW NLP
(NEURO-LINGUISTIC PROGRAMMING)
CAN TRANSFORM YOUR LIFE**

JULIET LEVER & PAUL ELISEO

EVOLVE YOUR MIND

Copyright 2023 © Paul Eliseo & Juliet Lever

The content in this book is designed to provide helpful information on the subjects discussed. This book is not meant to be used, nor should it be used, to diagnose or treat any medical condition. For diagnosis or treatment of any medical problem, consult your own physician. The publisher and authors are not responsible for any specific health or allergy needs that may require medical supervision and are not liable for any damages or negative consequences from any treatment, action, application or preparation, to any person reading or following the information in this book. References are provided for informational purposes only and do not constitute endorsement of any websites or other sources. Readers should be aware that the websites listed in this book may change and many people's names and identifying characteristics have been changed for privacy.

Copyright © 2023 by Evolve and Relaunch Pty Ltd
ISBN: 978-0-6453765-0-0
Editor: Emma Offler
No reproduction without permission. All rights reserved
www.evolveandrelaunch.com.au

The author and publishers have made all reasonable efforts to contact copyright-holders for permission, and apologise for any omissions or errors in the form of credits given. Any corrections required should be submitted in writing to info@evolveandrelaunch.com.au

Formatting by Happy Self Publishing
www.happyselfpublishing.com

Contents

Welcome 7
Before we begin 9

CHAPTER 1: Get in the driver's seat 23
CHAPTER 2: Power of intention 31
CHAPTER 3: We all see the world differently 43
CHAPTER 4: Learning the language of your mind .. 61
CHAPTER 5: Reprogramming yourself 75
CHAPTER 6: Emotions are energy in motion 85
CHAPTER 7: Changing your past 93
CHAPTER 8: Designing your future 105
CHAPTER 9: Keep evolving 113

Testimonials 121
References 129
About the authors 133
Notes 135

Welcome to Evolve Your Mind

Welcome. If you have chosen this book, you're probably curious about how you can learn ways to evolve your mind and start to explore your unconscious programs, habits and patterns.

You are about to explore the life-changing world of Neuro-Linguistic Programming (NLP) and learn how it can help you create transformation in your life.

This book has been co-authored by the founders and trainers of Evolve and Relaunch Education, Paul Eliseo and Juliet Lever and the intention of this book is to 'simplify' some of the most powerful NLP concepts. It's also designed to give you activities to help evolve your mind and understand what you can expect from studying with Evolve and Relaunch.

By reading this book and completing the activities at the end of each chapter, you will gain a deeper understanding of the modality and of yourself. Plus, you will be far more prepared for a live training (if and when you choose to study with Evolve and Relaunch!).

In this book you will discover new insights to help you understand certain concepts from NLP as well as be provided with self-reflection activities at the end of every chapter to dive deeper and help to consolidate your learnings.

To get the most value from this book we encourage you to head to our website at **www.evolveandrelaunch.com.au/evolveyourmind** to download our free interactive *Evolve Your Mind* PDF workbook with all the activities from this book to complete as you read. You will also find bonus videos and audios to watch and listen to which guide some of the processes in this book.

Special note: This book is not designed to replace the Evolved NLP live trainings. The experience of a live training with Evolve and Relaunch Education is dynamic and transformational in a way that cannot compare to words written on a page.

Keep Evolving,
Paul and Juliet

Before we begin…

Before we start this book we would like to share a few important background elements about NLP and provide you with some insight about how Paul and Juliet have personally transformed their lives using these skills.

What is NLP, and when was it developed?

NLP stands for Neuro-Linguistic Programming.

It was developed in the mid-1970s by its co-creators Richard Bandler, a computer engineer, and John Grinder, a linguistics professor. Together they were curious about whether they could reverse-engineer the processes the best therapists of their time were using to get profound results with their clients.

Because success leaves clues, they were able to model the therapists' communication (both verbal and non-verbal communication, language, tonality, gestures), intention and strategies in order to achieve positive outcomes. They wanted to create a system that could be replicated and repeated to allow anyone to follow and get the same outcomes. As a result they developed the tools and techniques that make up NLP to help humans create transformation in their lives.

However, NLP is not only useful for therapy, it also helps you adopt a mindset and methodology for success in life. The core concept is that any person who has achieved success in any area of life has done so by having a certain mindset or methodology. And this methodology can be modelled or replicated to create results. For example, people who have success in investing, health, relationships or business all have certain beliefs, values, habits and associations that help them to create their results. If we can replicate their beliefs, values and habits in ourselves then we can also replicate similar results in our own lives.

NLP is fundamentally built upon the concept of modelling. That is, finding what works in human behaviour and replicating it. In this book you will discover some models that Paul and Juliet have created to help their students get the most out of their trainings and understand NLP concepts at a deeper level. Whilst they aren't 'traditional NLP' models, they are based on the idea of modelling.

Before we begin...

Evolve and Relaunch Education has been teaching NLP and Hypnotherapy since the early 2000's and have constantly evolved and modernised the concepts in order to train a new generation of NLP Practitioners, some of whom are industry leaders in their own niche. Whether these Practitioners work with children, businesses, relationships, money or trauma issues, the training provided by Evolve and Relaunch helps bring the skills to life and makes them applicable in today's modern world.

The mindset of NLP is also about having an attitude of curiosity, and exploring the subjective nature of our world. That is to say, no two people experience the same version of reality. This book will encourage your curiosity about yourself, your programming, your beliefs and habits in order to help you transform in the process.

What is the mind and why do you even want to evolve it?

When most people are asked what the mind is, they usually get some sort of mental image of a brain. Although this is common, this isn't 100% accurate. The brain is in fact a part of the mind.

Daniel J Siegal MD defines the 'mind', as an '**emergent, self-organising, embodied, and relational process that regulates the flow of energy and information**.'

This flow occurs both within the body (including the brain), as well as in the sharing of energy and information between an individual and others and the environment in which the person lives.

By offering a definition of the mind, you can see how the mind is both within us and between us, within the body and the brain, and within the relational connections you have with other people and the world around you.

In this book the authors will also refer to the conscious and unconscious mind (or subconscious—the two terms are interchangeable). The main difference between the conscious and unconscious mind stems from the basic human functions and mental processes. Your conscious mind is in control of your rational and logical thinking whereas your unconscious mind is the part of you that manages your involuntary actions, unconscious patterns and habits.

Conscious mind	Unconscious mind
Logical and intellectual processes.	Physical functions and habits.
Decision making, planning.	Breathing, storehouse of memory, feelings, emotions, beliefs, gut instinct, attitudes.
Think of the ship's captain steering the ship and giving the orders.	Think of the ship itself, the crew, the sails, the wind and the sea. Everything supporting the ship captain to get to its destination.
Goal setter.	Goal getter.

Why do you want to evolve your mind?

One of Paul's favourite sayings is, 'in life we can either evolve by choice or by chance'. When people stop actively growing and evolving, they tend to unconsciously attract external challenges to force them to grow. These challenges can be random, haphazard and even unpleasant.

As an example, did you ever go on the dodgem cars as a child? What is the point of this ride? Essentially, it's to aimlessly drive around and wait for things to crash into you and react to the things other people do to you.

You constantly get knocked off your path and there is no real way to win or clear direction.

This is how most people live life—responding and reacting to 'accidents', bumping into things and people and having no set clear intention to move towards their goals.

On the other hand, if you make the decision to evolve by choice, you can direct the change and expansion as a conscious driver of your own life. This means you can step off the dodgem cars, stop letting the outside world knock you off your path and start getting on the right track for your desired direction in life.

In this book you will also learn the importance of evolving your mind because the quality of your life experience is a direct reflection of the quality of your thoughts and perceptions.

Before we begin...

PAUL'S STORY

First of all, thank you for being here and choosing the path that has led you to read this book. I know that if you are reading this book then you are ready to make changes in your life. I personally know how much NLP has transformed my life and the lives of the people I have been privileged to work with.

My journey into the world of mindset and hypnotherapy came from my own search for ways to handle what was happening to me. I had a challenging upbringing with my parents separating at a young age, changing schools and adjusting to a new family and siblings when my mother remarried. I felt lost, unsafe and alone a lot of the time. As I grew into a teenager these unresolved issues developed into insecurity and lack of confidence. I experienced social anxiety, regular panic attacks and also suffered physical symptoms like irritable bowel syndrome (IBS), sweats and black outs.

One day, my anxiety and social phobia got so bad, I couldn't leave the house. I tried for hours to go to a friend's house but just couldn't bring myself to walk out the front door. That day, I had a moment where I didn't recognise myself in the mirror. I realised that, as my fears grew bigger, my world was getting smaller and I was trapped inside a hell of my own creation.

Something needed to change.

So, I made a promise to myself to do whatever I could to find myself again.

I managed to convince myself to make my way out of the house, and found myself at the quietest place I could find—the local library. I started looking through sections in the library and a book caught my eye because it was about eating disorders, which was something my girlfriend was struggling with at the time. I thought I could learn something to help her and whilst the first chapter of the book related to her issue, when I flipped the pages to the second chapter, I was surprised to find it explained exactly what I was going through with irritable bowel syndrome. I didn't expect the book could help me too.

The chapter suggested I should keep a thought journal. So, I started writing down what I was thinking about every time I had a bout of IBS or anxiety, and soon started to realise that when my thoughts were about stressful situations in the future, my physical symptoms flared up. This was a massive lightbulb which led me to understand the power of my thoughts and the effect they were having on my body.

Before we begin...

It was from this point onwards I became obsessed with the mind-body connection and started learning NLP and self-hypnosis tools. These tools completely transformed what I thought was possible for myself and through my own transformation it also inspired me to start helping others.

I initially started my journey of helping others by becoming a personal trainer and helping people physically. After years of study and working with people, I became Personal Trainer of the Year for South Australia in 2008. But, after a while, I noticed that it didn't matter what exercises we used or how many reps and sets my clients did, no matter how well I designed their exercise program or helped them come up with the perfect nutrition plan for their lifestyle and goals, the results were all driven by their mindset. Whether they would stick to their programs and get results, sabotage or not even start was all based on their mental and emotional strength more so than their physical capacity.

So, I started studying NLP and hypnotherapy, seeing clients and even went on to became a trainer of these two modalities in my early 20s. I knew that the tools that helped me go from a nervous and anxious teenager afraid to leave his room to becoming the best trainer in the biggest gym in my city would be a total game changer for others if I could master the processes and pass on my knowledge. I felt disillusioned by many of the NLP trainings out there as they were more focused on what NLP is. I was always more focused on how NLP could help people.

The transformation is so much more powerful than the information so I modified and added to my courses to give people the most transformative and experiential learning experience possible.

My business originated as Evolve Mind and Body Coaching and has now evolved into Evolve and Relaunch Education with my beautiful partner in business and life, Juliet. I am thankful for living a life of meaning and purpose, helping people consciously release their programming and create what they want in life.

My passion is to make learning fun and safe. Yes, I promise my students corny dad jokes, but at the same time I have 100% intention and belief in everyone being able to overcome any obstacle they have in life. I look forward to meeting you at one of our trainings in future.

Keep evolving,
Paul

Before we begin...

JULIET'S STORY

Welcome and thank you for taking the time to read my journey of transformation. I honestly believe NLP and hypnotherapy are the most important skills any of us can learn in life.

By the time I had reached my mid-twenties I was feeling very stuck in life. I could even use the word 'trapped'.

On the surface, things looked great—I was married and had a successful career with a well-paying job, but deep down I wasn't happy. I had no passion in my life and I experienced daily debilitating anxiety that I just couldn't get rid of. I was trapped in a life of my own 'unconscious' creation.

I had a series of wake-up calls in the form of anxiety/panic attacks, binge drinking and some hard truths (that I shared in my first book) which helped me realise I needed to make a change.

So, on my 27th birthday in 2013, I started keeping my very first journal. I had written diaries as a child but these were more in depth and about how I was feeling. I wrote in my journal morning and night for one week. At the end of the seven days I re-read all of my journal entries and something fascinating jumped out at me: I counted the word 'overwhelmed' over 20 times. I thought to myself 'wow, maybe that's got something to do with why I feel so anxious and… overwhelmed!'

So, I wrote a big list of everything I was feeling overwhelmed about and wrote a 'C' next to everything on the list I could Change. Then, I wrote an 'A' next to everything I couldn't change and had to Accept.

Change or Accept, those are our two options in life.

It immediately halved the list. Next to the items I could Change, I listed 2-3 things that I could do about it, actions I could take. Immediately I felt in control of my life and the anxiety subsided and this was the beginning of me discovering the power of our thoughts over our emotions.

In 2013, I ended my passionless marriage and set out to follow my desire of becoming a life coach. Along the way, I discovered that many successful people had studied NLP and hypnotherapy and so I knew I wanted to learn more about these. I even had a hypnotherapy healing session which helped me understand the root of my anxiety and released a fear of abandonment. After meeting Paul in 2014 and studying hypnotherapy and NLP, I started my coaching and retreat business, Relaunch My Life, and wrote my best-selling self-help book of the same name in 2017. (I would absolutely recommend grabbing a copy of my book Relaunch My Life which is a guide to help you find and follow your purpose in life).

I started teaching NLP in 2018 and Paul and I joined our businesses together as Evolve and Relaunch Education from then on. I am grateful to have created an entirely different life for myself than the life I was living unconsciously as a result of my programming and fear of abandonment.

From clearing these things, I honestly have NLP and hypnotherapy to thank for the life I have now created for myself, a life that is full of love, purpose and meaning. My passion is helping people find the courage and confidence to change any aspect of their life, because I know just how stuck and lost I was and I know there is strength and light in you that is ready to be uncovered.

What I love about our trainings is they don't make you anything you aren't already. They help you show more of your true self to the world—the real you beneath all the layers of programming that were never you to begin with.

That's what I'm passionate about: helping people reconnect with their true selves and create a life of their own conscious creation.

With love and respect,
Juliet x

Now that we have both shared with you how NLP has personally transformed our lives and why it's so important to evolve your mind, let's explore how NLP can start changing yours… today.

CHAPTER 1

GET IN THE DRIVER'S SEAT

> *'You are personally responsible for everything in your life, once you become aware that you are personally responsible for everything in your life.'*
> **– Dr Bruce Lipton**

Have you ever found yourself making excuses for not achieving something you wanted to in life?

Have you ever blamed someone or something else for why you have or have not achieved something in your life?

Are you getting all of the results you truly want in all areas of your life?

If you are, that's fantastic—and you'll experience even more improved results through the process of understanding and applying the concepts within this book.

However, if you are currently not getting the results you want, you may not have realised that you have unconsciously been giving your power over to someone or something else without even realising it.

In this section you will discover a new way of thinking that will allow you to take control of your life so that you can get in the driver's seat, tap into your internal resources, stop blaming the outside world and start claiming your power.

It can be easy to fall into an unconscious habit of blaming others or making excuses for why things are the way they are rather than look within.

Blaming others disempowers you in the process. This is because, the moment you blame someone or something else, you give your power over to that person saying they are the reason your life isn't the way you want it to be. This consequently also shuts down your ability to influence the outcome.

Everyone has blamed others at some point in their lives, whether it's your parents and upbringing, the government, technology or even children.

For example, some people might say, 'My whole family is overweight so that's why I am as well.' Some may say, 'My parents weren't good with money so I'm not either, and I was never taught how to manage my money.' Others may say, 'It's my partner's fault I am unhappy.'

The stories you tell yourself become a suggestion to your unconscious mind. So, whatever the story has been up until now, know that you can change your stories and create more useful suggestions for yourself.

From an NLP perspective, this idea of changing your stories and empowering yourself by taking ownership of your experiences in life is known as the 'empowerment' model and being 'at cause' for your life.

The Law of Cause-and-Effect states that for every cause, there is an equal effect. This is also similar to Newton's third law, *'For every action, there is an equal and opposite reaction'.*

Being at cause is taking on the perspective of how you *can* do or change something.

Being at effect is only considering and being stuck in all the ways you *can't*.

If you want to step into the driver's seat of your life (which you naturally must want to do if you are reading this book) and steer yourself towards better results, then you need to make the decision to start living 'at cause'.

This model is also often referred to as 'above the line' or 'below the line' thinking.

Above the line thinking:
Ownership
Accountability
Results

vs

Below the line thinking:
Blame
Excuses
Denial

ACTIVITY:
Write down each of the different areas of your life and where you may not be fully at cause. Look at your results in your health, finances, relationships and career.

Ask yourself, what would happen if you decided to take your power back and step into cause in these areas?

_____
_____
_____
_____

STUDENT STORY:

One of our students, Stacey, was kind enough to share her story with us. In 2017, after a lifetime of unresolved struggles such as anxiety, binge drinking, depression and abuse, Stacey experienced what she would call a complete nervous breakdown. She had suicidal tendencies and was almost hospitalised. She developed tremors and was unable to function. After many scans and tests, the specialists told her there was something wrong with her but they didn't know what exactly. Twenty-two lesions were found on her brain and she was also diagnosed with Functional Neurological Disorder (essentially, she was told that her brain wasn't properly communicating with her body). Stacey experienced daily head tremors and at times even forgot how to do basic tasks like driving her car and how to co-ordinate her legs to walk—her body started shutting down. Her family accepted the worst, and even renovated their home to widen the doorframes to allow for her future need for a wheelchair.

After the specialists had no answers for her, Stacey made a decision to try to change her situation through natural approaches. She studied functional nutrition, practiced meditation and visualisation of her brain repairing and came across the work of one of our Master Practitioner students, Kim Morrison. Incredibly, after booking in for a breakthrough session and having her first four-hour coaching session, Stacey's head tremors halved. Stacey attributes this to finally releasing the root cause of emotional issues she had which were causing her to physically carry shame, fear and many other emotions in her body.

After experiencing these incredible changes, Stacey then went on to study NLP, hypnotherapy and Master Practitioner with Evolve & Relaunch in 2021/2022 and she told us during Master Practitioner she felt like she 'met her true self' for the first time in her life.

Stacey adds, 'I wish I knew how to explain to people just how important it is to do all of Evolve and Relaunch Education's trainings. They helped me put the pieces together, the pain that has been let go in my body is incredible and I now have no symptoms and no longer even say that I have a brain condition."

This is an incredible example of how the ideas taught in Evolve and Relaunch Education's courses helped Stacey truly take her power back and use the full capacity of her internal resources to evolve her mind. It also demonstrates her decision to get in the driver's seat of her life and take full responsibility for her own healing.

CHAPTER 2

THE POWER OF INTENTION

'When your intention is clear, so is the way.'
– Alan Cohen

Have you ever wanted to understand the mechanics behind creating what you want and manifesting more effectively?

Are you curious about why some days it can seem like no matter what you do, nothing gets done and other days, you effortlessly achieve so much with less time and energy?

Would it be useful to know why some goals and dreams come to reality and others seem elusive, regardless of your effort?

While this is not a book specifically about manifestation, one of the foundations of NLP is the idea that your thoughts and perceptions create your reality (which will be covered in more depth in chapters 4 and 5). Some people think they need to learn how to manifest but the truth is you are constantly manifesting based on your thoughts and perceptions. This means you are taking the quantum probabilities of infinite potential and collapsing into what you perceive as a problem.

But you have infinite potential and also infinite ways of perceiving the world.

Based on your thoughts and feelings, you can be manifesting what appear to be issues and problems in your life if you aren't careful about what you are focusing on.

While on the quest to understanding how human beings create their reality, Paul discovered that, no matter what level of awareness one has, everyone is creating their own reality.

Whether reality is assessed through the lens of psychology (through our beliefs, values and cognitive biases), spiritually/energetically (through the law of attraction/law of vibration), or physically (through neurotransmitters and cell receptors craving chemical responses that distort our perceptions of reality to re-enforce emotional addictions), this idea is consistent.

The following model Paul has designed which blends all of these perspectives, enables you to understand how you can manifest what you want in life and leads to dramatic increases in your ability to consciously create your reality.

Although this model is not a traditional NLP concept in itself, Paul developed the model to help our students apply this concept in their life to get better results with themselves and their clients.

The power of intention

Evolve Manifestation Model™

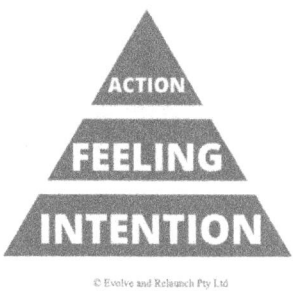

Step 1: Intention

The first step in the Evolve Manifestation Model™ is to get clear on your intention.

We have all heard we need to start with why. This is because your intention is the *why*. Thinking about your intention forms the electrical signal that primes your nervous system for a response. When you are clear and concise with your intention, you can filter your reality for what you want and your Reticular Activation System (RAS) actually starts drawing people and places to us to support you in creating the outcome. The thought signal is the first step of manifestation and creating what you desire. So often in life people are not clear about what they want. If you aren't clear about what you want to achieve then it's as though you are going on a journey without setting a clear direction on the GPS. This means you are more likely to go around in circles and never get clear on where you are going. This means you also may not know if you are moving in the right direction and this is one of the major reasons for lack of progress.

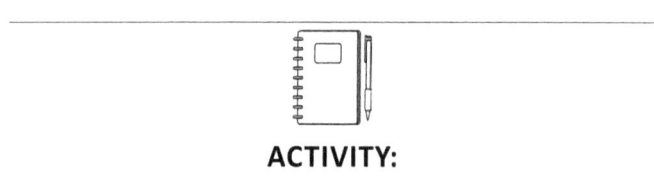

ACTIVITY:
Take a moment to consider your intention for reading this book.

How specifically do you want to apply your intention, and what specific change/s do you want to make? Consider and write your intention in a key area of your life:

_____
_____
_____
_____

Step 2: Feeling/E-motion

Once you are clear on your intention, you need to combine that intention with a supportive feeling.

So, the feeling (energy in motion) that supports our intention is the magnetic component of the electro-magnetic field that you create once your intention (electric) and your emotion (magnetic) are combined. The thought fires electrical impulses through your neurons which release neuro-transmitters (chemical messengers) at the synaptic gap.

Synaptic Transmission

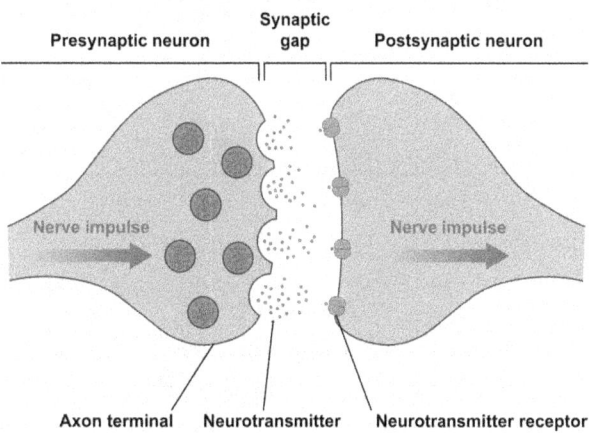

These neuro-transmitters bathe every cell of your body and help carry the signal throughout the nervous system, creating your emotions and a chemical cascade that occurs with every thought you have.

Once activated in your body together, emotions further shift your physiology, psychology and bio-energetics to either prime you to pursue, pause or even cause you to panic and run away from want you want. The outcome is based upon the perception of the emotion that is released with the thought. If you have supportive and positive emotion behind your intention, that will dramatically influence your ability to manifest your desires. If your underlying emotion is negative, it won't enable you to attract what you desire and will actually attract the opposite of what you intend to create.

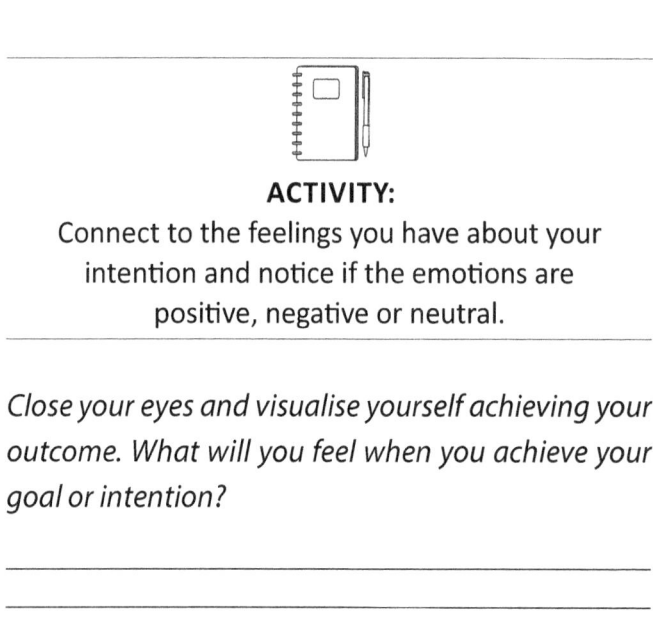

ACTIVITY:
Connect to the feelings you have about your intention and notice if the emotions are positive, negative or neutral.

Close your eyes and visualise yourself achieving your outcome. What will you feel when you achieve your goal or intention?

_____
_____
_____
_____

The optimal feeling you want to achieve when using this model and thinking about your goals is to experience the state of gratitude.

That is, to imagine your goal/intention has already happened, and you are experiencing it as though it is already done, then you can feel the feelings/emotions that come with its achievement. This sends the signal to your body/mind that it has already happened and that it is real. As your body/mind doesn't know the difference between real and imagined it brings forth whatever it is you intended to manifest.

In life when you are taking a new path or trying something new (such as starting a business, going on a date or trying a new form of study) it's natural to experience feelings of fear, uncertainty and even doubt. This is a great thing as it indicates you are growing and trying something new. But, as humans are hard wired to avoid pain, often these emotions prevent you from taking new pathways. It's more comfortable to avoid something new.

At Evolve and Relaunch Education we have developed a simple reframe to support our students when they study with us to get used to (and even embrace) these feelings. We call these feelings, the Feelings of Growth, or shortened to the 'FOG'.

Learn to embrace the Feelings Of Growth (FOG) as it means you are learning, growing and evolving.

Step 3: Action

Once you have a clear intention and aligned and supportive emotion, then you want to take action. Unfortunately, it is common to take action before getting clear on steps 1 and 2 first (or take action when your feeling isn't aligned which results in wasted energy).

You have probably had the experience of being at work and feeling like you are spending a lot of time and energy but nothing is getting done. But you would also have had the experience when you paused for a moment and got clear on exactly what needed to be done and how you wanted it to be (set an intention), captured the feeling of it already being done (feeling/emotion), then took action and achieved more in 20-30 minutes than you sometimes do in a day!

So, in summary you want to ensure you have alignment in your intention and feelings before you take the third and final step, action.

Example: When Juliet first started her coaching business, she worked with women who wanted to start their own businesses—and she witnessed this manifestation model first hand. She can recall one particular client who told her at the start of their first session, 'I want to start my own business!' When Juliet explored the underlying feelings around her intention, her client told her she was feeling fear, uncertainty and nervousness.

Needless to say, the client wasn't taking any empowered action towards starting her business. Within only two sessions using NLP and hypnotherapy techniques, Juliet helped her client shift her feelings about her ability to take action in her business from fear and uncertainty to clarity and a deep sense of knowing. The action her client took as a result was aligned, confident and simple. And she even started attracting people to help her with her business!

The world responds to the energy and emotion behind the things we say we want to do.

ACTIVITY:
Notice what actions you have been taking in your life (or inaction) and consider if this is because you haven't become clear on your intention or your emotions are not supporting it.

Chapter activity: Pause and consider something you are wanting to create in your future, and what emotions you have around it and what actions you have/haven't been taking.

_____

_____

_____

_____

_____

CHAPTER 3

WE ALL SEE THE WORLD DIFFERENTLY

> *'People will be who you need them to be, so you can see what you need to see.'*
> **– Paul Eliseo**

A few years ago, Juliet was teaching an NLP training in Perth, Australia. She stayed at an AirBnb nearby which was quite modern apart from one feature: there was a big split system air-conditioning unit high up on the wall in the living room. When she turned it on, the filters opened up and she noticed that they were COATED with a thick layer of dust. They hadn't been cleaned... probably ever.

It made her think about the way we all filter our reality. We filter our reality, but most of us have never been shown how to clean the filters of our perception... and as a result everything we experience is being filtered through the congested layers of the past. Just like the air in the room had to pass through the filter and getting caught in the dust, your current life experience is passing through your unresolved mental/emotional experiences.

Our realities are all so unique. One of the simplest ways of explaining this fact is through a model called the NLP Communication Model.

For example, take a moment to notice that you are reading this book right now and you can see things in the room or space you are in around the book too. You can also feel the book or reading device in your hands. You may be able to hear some noises right now. You may even be able to smell or taste something. You are constantly taking in the outside world through your five senses.

These five senses are visual (sight), auditory (hearing), kinaesthetic (touch), olfactory (smell) and gustatory (taste).

You take in all information about the outside world through these senses and you actually receive an immense amount of information. In fact, it's too much data for you to take in consciously, so, you have to filter some of it out to make sense of the world.

Studies have shown that you consciously filter for about 134 bits of information per second, whereas your unconscious mind is able to take in about 2,000,000 bits of information. That means you consciously absorb only 0.000067% of what your unconscious mind can. That's a huge difference and demonstrates the incredible power of your unconscious mind!

Imagine for a moment there are 2,000,000 toothpicks falling from the sky. If you were to take 134 toothpicks from that group and call that reality, that would be far from the truth. But because that's all you can filter for consciously, that's all you experience. No two people are ever filtering for the exact same 134 toothpicks (or exact same reality).

If you had to process all 2,000,000 bits of information per second, you would be overloaded! So, in order to make sense of the world you have to filter it. The process of filtering is done instantly, and we do this by deleting, distorting and generalising the information that comes to us.

Now, we all filter for different bits of information based on a few determining factors. The way we delete, distort and generalise is based on our programming. More specifically, our beliefs, our attitudes, strategies, values, experiences, memories, meta-programs (our meta-programs are some of our deepest unconscious sorting filters) and even the way we perceive time/space/energy/matter. Your filters of perception can get a little distorted if you have never cleaned them out, just like in the example of the air conditioner described earlier.

This is so fascinating because it also highlights why two people can have very different reactions or experiences of the exact same event.

For example, let's imagine a beach scene. A surf life saver will notice the way the waves are moving and if there are any rip tides. They will notice if there are any children in the area and if they have their parents with them or nearby, and they will especially notice if the people in the water are struggling or look comfortable. Someone going fishing may be looking at the tide levels and what the season is. A surfer will be looking for the wind, the waves and how busy the water is in general. A sunbaker will look at the cloud cover and the available sand. A dog walker will notice the other dogs and not even consider the water, unless their dog likes to go for a swim.

It's the same reality, but no two people filter for the same version of reality.

Everyone sees the world differently based on what is important to them and their filters of perception. Your perceptions create your reality. And your perceptions are creating a self-fulfilling prophecy.

There are three main ways we filter reality based on our values and programs:

1. **Delete**
   Paul used to work as a personal trainer in one of the largest gyms in Adelaide. At the time he overheard a lot of struggling personal trainers say 'there are no clients out there'. By holding this belief, the personal trainers simply didn't

see how many potential clients there were—therefore, they 'deleted' them! Paul didn't share this belief and didn't delete all the potential customers from his world. He would walk out onto the gym floor and see people performing bad technique in their weights exercises or struggling on cardio machines and he would start chatting with them. Soon enough, they would become clients. He was a fully booked personal trainer who won Personal Trainer of the Year for South Australia whereas other trainers who deleted out all the opportunities came and went.

You have to delete information out of your reality for efficiency, because you can't consciously absorb everything. However, sometimes you delete things out that you actually want in your life. You will always find what you filter for as you have what's called a confirmation bias, which can be either positive or negative.

Thankfully with our Evolved NLP and Time Line Therapy® techniques you can learn how to shift subconscious beliefs like these so you can start to filter for the abundance of customers, great partners, financial abundance and other opportunities that do exist in the world.

2. **Distort**

    Have you ever sent an email or an SMS to someone and they have misinterpreted the meaning? Or have you ever not received a reply from someone and made up a story in your head about how you offended them, or they don't like you?

    This is an example of distortion. Distorting your reality is a useful skill which allows you to be creative, to dream and to set goals. However, based on negative past experiences, you can easily make assumptions. Your distortions can cause problems that don't even exist if you aren't careful.

3. **Generalise**

    Your ability to chunk information and previously learnt concepts together helps you to learn quickly and is a useful skill for processing information. However, generalisations can also cause you to filter in ways that are not useful for creating what you want in life. An example of a generalisation could be, 'because I tried a few diets,

We all see the world differently

that means I'll never be able to lose weight' or 'ALL men/women/people are liars'.

For a moment, think about the fact that, every single second of the day, everyone is taking information in and filtering it and every single person filters their version of reality differently.

Because once you delete, distort and generalise, you form what is called an 'internal representation' of your experience of reality inside our mind. An internal representation is a mental picture with sounds and feelings, often accompanied with some self-talk.

This is illustrated by the Reality Creating Model below. This shows how you are always perceiving external events and filtering them in a split second. These filters create your internal representations.

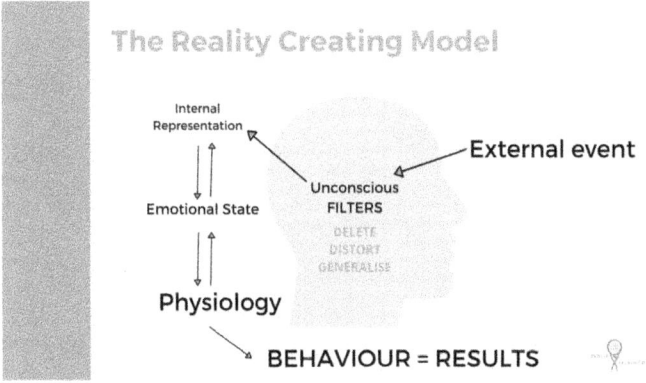

This running internal experience influences how you feel and then the actions you take in life.

Your physiology and emotional state can also influence the way you filter your internal representations.

For example, ***observe your physiology right now and shift into a hunched over posture with a frown upon your face. Try to feel ecstatic.***

It's challenging, isn't it?

Now, ***smile and look up and reach your arms out to the sky and try to feel miserable.***

It's almost impossible for you to feel miserable whilst adopting this posture.

This is a simple and quick demonstration of how your physiology can impact your mood and perceptions.

This is another example of the way your filters determine your reality.

We all see the world differently

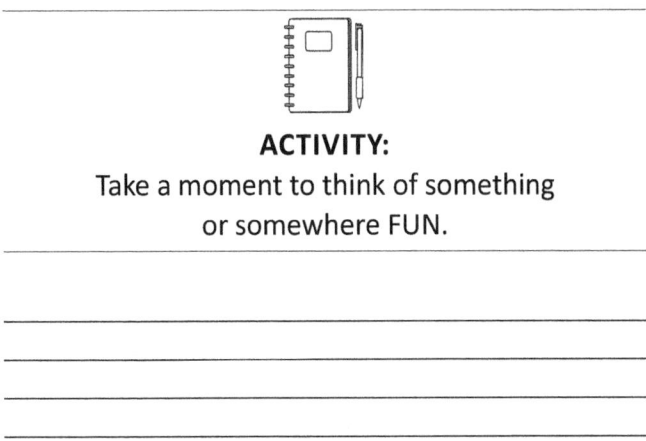

ACTIVITY:
Take a moment to think of something or somewhere FUN.

_____
_____
_____
_____

If you aren't used to searching for fun/positive times in life it may take a moment to find something. But even if it takes you a little while, there will be something to find! In thinking about something FUN, you would have had a certain concept in your mind (a mental image - which is also known as an internal representation in NLP terms).

Notice this concept of FUN for a moment.

What comes to mind when you think of something or somewhere FUN to you?

What do you see, hear, feel, taste, smell or say to yourself when you think about that?

See: _____

Hear: _____

Feel: _____

Taste: _____

Smell: _____

Say to yourself: _____

If you asked a room full of people that question ('what comes to mind when I say the word fun?'), every single person would have a different description and association to that word.

Each person would have an entirely different label and experience based on the way they delete, distort and generalise reality.

Note: Each person would also have an entirely different representation for the word 'fun' which would also indicate their values. For example, someone who has their highest value as business might think fun is landing their first high paying client. Someone whose highest value is family might think fun is a family trip to the beach. Our values are some of our deepest unconscious filters, and we all have a different set of values. Most conflicts in life occur due to a conflict of

We all see the world differently

values because it's hard to understand someone else's actions when they have a very different set of values to you. This is something we explore, and actually spend several days on in our Master Practitioner of NLP training as our values are one of our deepest unconscious filters.

Now, the word FUN is one linguistic representation.

It's one word.

What if you changed the tonality of that word?

Say FUN in a sarcastic tone.
Now say FUN in a monotone voice.
Now say FUN as if you are a clown at a circus.

The tonality of the way you use your words has a massive influence on your filters of perception. In fact, some research has shown that only 7% of your communication is the words you use. The rest is the tone of voice and way you say it (physiology and body language).

When you communicate with someone you use hundreds, even thousands of words.

And if each single word has so many variations to each human being, how do you ever truly know what is going on inside someone else's mind?

Through the study of NLP and our trainings you start to develop the skill of curiosity and also learn to never assume.

You will learn to ask the people you are speaking with what is happening inside their mind rather than assume that you know what they mean when you communicate with them.

One thing to be aware of is that whenever you are communicating to someone you are always influencing their internal representation.

For example, if you read these words: *don't think about a pink cat stretching on top of a white piano*, you would probably have visualised this.

Similarly, if you felt nervous and someone said to you 'don't be worried, it will all be okay', this will influence your internal representation and add the feeling of worry to your nervous experience.

Therefore, in order to create the best results in your life you always want to focus on WHAT you do want instead of NOT what you don't want. Focus your language on WHAT instead of NOT.

Often people have developed a habit of talking about the things they don't want in life. For example, 'oh, I just don't want to feel stressed out anymore' or 'I don't want to be overweight'.

This actually forms the internal representation (remember, your internal representation is the mental picture as well as sounds, smells, tastes, feelings, and even self-talk) of precisely what you don't want and sends mixed messages to your unconscious mind. So, if you think 'I want to be healthy' you will form an internal representation of what you DO want and what healthy looks/sounds/feels like to you.

So, start focusing on what you want, and articulating it clearly. Focus on WHAT *instead* of NOT. Focus on what you want.

Because you don't see the world as it is, you see the world as you are.

Chapter activity: Flip your NOTs to WHATs so you are sending clear instructions to your unconscious mind. This will help your captain (conscious mind) to send clear instructions to your crew (unconscious mind). Instead of focusing your energy on what you don't want, think about all of the major areas of your life and what you do want.

_____
_____
_____
_____

For example, in terms of your health—instead of saying, 'I do not want to eat Tim Tams anymore', which is the equivalent of the ship captain yelling out, 'don't go to Tim Tam Island!'—all the crew hear down below in the deck is, 'Tim Tams …. roger that!' and before you know it, you're reaching for another Tim Tam.

So, flip it to what you do want to ensure your message gets received clearly and the captain is giving clear orders to the crew: 'I eat healthy, balanced meals of meat, vegetables' etc. The clearer and more specific, the better. The crew says, 'roger that, captain' and start directing its sails towards that instruction with ease.

Instead of: I don't want to be lazy' (the crew hear, 'time to be lazy—roger that!')

Flip to: I train 3 x per week with weights and walk every day for 45 minutes ('roger that, captain', and the crew starts directs its sails towards that instruction).

Naturally, you would also want to explore and align your underlying beliefs and values as we do in our Evolved NLP Practitioner trainings to support these actions, but at the very least setting a clear direction is an important step in evolving.

We all see the world differently

Take a moment to reflect and fill in the rest of these:

Health
Do not want: _____
Want: _____

Relationship
Do not want: _____
Want: _____

Finances
Do not want: _____
Want: _____

Career/Purpose
Do not want: _____
Want: _____

Study/Growth
Do not want: _____
Want: _____

Other _____
Do not want:_____
Want: _____

CHAPTER 4

LEARNING THE LANGUAGE OF YOUR MIND

'Allow yourself to see what you don't allow yourself to see.'
– Milton H. Erickson

This chapter is a deeper exploration into the most powerful part of your mind—your unconscious mind.

Whether you have heard about your unconscious mind or not, this chapter intends to illustrate the power of this part of you and how to communicate more effectively with it. That is, learning the language of your mind and how to work with yourself, rather than against yourself.

This chapter is split into three sections:

1. Understanding your unconscious mind
2. Speaking with your unconscious mind; and
3. Change your unconscious mind, change your life

1. Understanding your unconscious mind

One of our favourite analogies is the idea that your conscious mind acts like a ship captain—it is at the helm of the ship, giving orders. The conscious mind is the part of you that decides to set a goal, start a diet, make a change in your life.

The unconscious mind (also sometimes referred to as the subconscious) is the ship supporting that captain. It's also the crew, the sails, the wind, the ocean, even the conditions supporting that ship to get where it wants to go.

Many people spend all their time consciously trying to change, but that's only about as useful as telling the captain to simply yell louder.

Instead of trying to create change from a conscious level, what if you could tap into your unconscious mind and ensure all your crew are rowing in the same direction? That's what our courses help people to do. They help you create rapport between your conscious and unconscious mind so that what you say and what you do aligns.

You may have experienced many challenges or obstacles in your life up until now. So many, that your crew may have completely stopped listening to your captain.

That is to say, your unconscious mind has stopped listening to you.

This is particularly evident in any areas of your life where you may want a particular outcome and yet your actions and habits are doing something completely different. For example, someone might consciously say they want to lose weight and yet find themselves unconsciously/habitually snacking on ice cream and sweets. This can be an indication that there is an unconscious program and belief system running a very different program to the conscious desires. There could even be an underlying belief that 'it's hard to lose weight' or 'I'll never be happy' that could be directing these unconscious programs.

Often clients and students share with us that their families used food as a way of connecting and showing love for one another growing up. So, sometimes when people try to lose weight, they have had an unconscious protection mechanism that would kick in—that if they rejected food by losing weight, they would also unconsciously be rejecting their family.

You will always live in alignment with your unconscious beliefs and desires, whether they are helpful or not.

The good news is that if the beliefs you are carrying are not aligned with what you consciously want to create then *it is possible to change them*. And with an attitude of curiosity, you can start to explore your underlying beliefs, programs and associations to create change in your direction.

2. Speaking with your unconscious mind

One of the areas we explore in our trainings are the key aspects (also called the 'prime directives') of your unconscious mind and how it operates. This is an eye-opener to truly understand how your powerhouse mind works. Here are some of the most interesting ways to work with and more deeply understand your unconscious mind:

i. **Your unconscious mind does not process negatives.** It is very simple and literal and will form mental images that become a suggestion to your unconscious mind. The example provided in the last chapter, *'Don't think of a pink cat stretching out on top of a white piano'* is a perfect display of how all language influences your unconscious mind. Once you are aware of this, you can understand how to speak with yourself to create the outcomes of what you want.

For example, someone who says, 'I just don't want to put on weight again' is creating the internal picture of themselves putting on weight because the unconscious mind doesn't process 'don't'. Or if someone thinks 'I don't want to attract another bad relationship' or 'I don't want to be stressed' they are in fact unconsciously filtering for it.

A simple way to reframe this pattern if you catch yourself speaking about what you don't want is to say, 'Okay, so, what is it that I do want?' and quickly re-state it. This was explained in the 'What' instead of 'Not' concept in the previous chapter.

ii. **Your unconscious mind loves clear instructions.** In fact, the simpler, the better. You may have no idea just how many mixed signals you are giving to your unconscious mind.

For example, a lot of people say they want something, and yet their unconscious feelings are the exact opposite of the thing they want, therefore, their action will be unclear. As explained in the *Power of Intention* in Chapter 2, your thoughts and feelings need to align in order to create aligned action. For example, many people feel guilt, fear of loss, uncertainty and even shame when they think about money. They might set a financial goal but while these unresourceful thoughts and feelings are associated they are unlikely to take action.

In our trainings we help our students align their thoughts with their feelings to provide clarity to the unconscious mind so they can achieve the things they truly want.

iii. Here are a few more of the key prime directives of your unconscious mind you may not have been conscious of. We explore these more deeply in our NLP and hypnotherapy courses.

The unconscious mind:

- STORES your memories
- Is the domain of the EMOTIONS (if someone is in an emotional state, they are accessing their subconscious)
- ORGANISES all your memories
- REPRESSES memories with unresolved negative emotion
- PRESENTS repressed memories for resolution
- May KEEP repressed emotions repressed for protection
- RUNS the body (for example, the central nervous system, respiratory systems etc—you don't have to consciously operate these)

- Has a blueprint of the body in perfect health and its ideal condition
- PRESERVES and maintains the integrity of the body
- Is a highly MORAL being (the morality you were taught and accepted)
- Enjoys serving, NEEDS CLEAR ORDERS to follow
- CONTROLS and MAINTAINS all perceptions
- RECEIVES and TRANSMITS perceptions to the conscious mind
- Generates, stores, distributes and transmits ENERGY
- Maintains INSTINCTS and generates HABITS
- INSTALLS habits after repetition
- Is programmed to continually SEEK more and more
- FUNCTIONS best as a whole integrated unit
- Is SYMBOLIC
- Takes everything PERSONALLY
- Works on the PRINCIPLE OF LEAST EFFORT—the path of least resistance
- Does not process NEGATIVES

You may not have fully appreciated just how powerful your unconscious mind is up until now.

Being able to truly connect, communicate and align with your unconscious mind is going to change your life and results dramatically.

3. Change your unconscious mind, change your life

It is one thing to become aware of a pattern or belief that is held in your unconscious mind but it is another entirely to change it and clear it.

To give a crude metaphor, this is the difference between 'stepping in shit' or 'cleaning up shit'.

You don't want to just become aware of your shit—you need to clean it up too!

When you learn how to swiftly and effectively discover the root cause of stored emotions and limiting beliefs in our trainings, you will be amazed at the wisdom and intelligence of your unconscious mind. Within minutes a lifetime of limitation can be released once the unconscious mind has been supported to shift the belief at the root cause.

Your unconscious mind will only let go of a belief, emotion or limitation if you have learnt all you need to about it. This is because one of the prime directives of your unconscious mind is that it is always trying to protect you. This is an important key because often people think their unconscious mind is working against them, but it is always working for you. Sometimes this hard wired program to protect you actually stops you from the things you want.

STUDENT STORY:

One of our students, Wez, realised he had a massive limiting belief holding him back around his self-worth. This subconscious belief of not being good enough was causing issues in his life by him not taking steps towards building his business and it also created self-sabotage patterns, including taking drugs.

Wez was able to clear the root cause of this limiting belief in our NLP Practitioner training and set goals and started working with paying clients. He has gone on to study further levels of trainings with us and his life has now changed because he is more congruent, aligned in his self-belief and manifests with zero resistance.'

ACTIVITY:
Take a moment to look at the things you want in the previous chapter. Notice if you are giving clear or mixed signals to your crew.

For the different areas of your life, what are your thoughts, feelings and associations about these intentions? When you think about it, do you get a clear image? What do you say to yourself and what emotions arise when you think about this goal?

Health outcome
Mental picture_____
Emotions _____
Thoughts _____

Relationship outcome
Mental picture_____
Emotions _____
Thoughts _____

Finance outcome
Mental picture_____
Emotions _____
Thoughts _____

Career/Purpose outcome
Mental picture_____
Emotions _____
Thoughts _____

Study/Growth outcome
Mental picture_____
Emotions _____
Thoughts _____

Other desired outcome
Mental picture_____
Emotions _____
Thoughts _____

In our NLP training you also learn a lot more about your unconscious mind as well as the structure of language and how we actually construct problems in our thinking 'linguistically'. We learn how to expand our communication into hypnotic language and abstraction and then deep into detail and clarity. We also explore how to think around, above and beneath problems, so we can literally 'outthink' our problems.

Consider Albert Einstein's famous quote: *'We can't solve problems by using the same thinking we used when we created them.'*

CHAPTER 5

REPROGRAMMING YOURSELF

> *'The way our brain is wired, we only see what we believe is possible. We match patterns that already exist within ourselves through conditioning.'*
> **– Candace Pert**

Who programmed you?

Did you consciously choose all the belief patterns that you hold?

Probably not.

In fact, none of us did.

Usually, our biggest programmers were our parents, sometimes our siblings and grandparents or even early childhood teachers. Even if our parents weren't in the picture, that in itself can be a part of our programming too.

Living life with other people's programming is like being handed a map for an out-of-date world that doesn't exist anymore. And even if your parents did the best they possibly could, sometimes the programming you received from them during your childhood doesn't fit the world we live in today.

Thankfully you can learn tools to upgrade the maps of your software. This way you no longer need to use bulky old street directories, and you can update to Google Maps in order to get where you want to go in your life.

Our imprint period is the period between the ages of 0-7 where you actually didn't have a filter for your conscious mind. You were like a sponge—

absorbing all the emotions and beliefs of the people around you. This can be useful to help you adopt useful strategies and beliefs such as 'I should always try my best'. However, often the beliefs you picked up through misinterpreting events could be unuseful.

Imagine for a moment one day your parents were running late for work and didn't have time to listen to you tell them about what happened at school the day before. You may have formed a belief that 'I am not important' which over an entire lifetime could have manifested as 'I'm not worthy'. An isolated event or several events stacked over time can form a belief.

Think about one of your favourite outfits or shoes you had as a small child. They fit you as a child, but if you tried to squeeze into them today it would look pretty ridiculous—and feel very restricting! This is what it's like to carry around beliefs you received in your childhood. They were useful at the time but after a lifetime they can become limiting and very uncomfortable.

A lot of the direct suggestions you received in your childhood were also because your parents were living in a very different time to when you are (and so were your grandparent's who programmed them). So, sometimes you can still be carrying around a belief that you have well and truly outgrown, or they never really 'fit' at all. Examples of suggestions you might have heard growing up are: 'children should be seen and not heard' and 'you have to work hard to earn money' and 'it's not okay to be angry/upset'.

One of the presuppositions of NLP is 'everyone is doing the best they can with the resources they have available'. This can be a useful reminder to take ownership for the programming you received. Because it's not anyone's fault for how you were programmed (because they too were programmed by someone), but it's your responsibility and opportunity to reprogram yourself once you have the tools to know how.

Take a moment to consider the primary sources of programming that you experienced. You could think of this as an unconscious blueprint that you're carrying around.

- *What did your mother think/say/do about health and wellness?*

　　_____
　　_____

- *What did your father think/say/do about health and wellness?*

  _____
  _____

- *What did your mother think/say/do about money?*

  _____
  _____

- *What did your father think/say/do about money?*

  _____
  _____

- *What did your mother think/say/do in regards to your father?*

  _____
  _____

- *What did your father think/say/do in regards to your mother?*

  _____
  _____

- *What did your mother think/say/do about work?*

  _____
  _____

- *What did your father think/say/do about work?*

  _____
  _____

- *You can also ask all of these questions about your grandparents, siblings and friends during childhood as they all played a part in your imprinting.*

  _____
  _____

Now, consider your answers to all of these questions and notice, how has that shaped how you are in your life?

Now explore a little further. Consider your answers to these questions or statements:

Life is_____
_____

Money is_____
_____

Work is_____
_____

Success is_____
_____

I am not _____

I never _____

I can't _____

I shouldn't _____

I won't _____

People are _____

Relationships are _____

These are only a few select statements, however, you may have become conscious of some blueprints running programs that aren't creating the results you desire in life.

In our Evolved NLP Practitioner training you will discover tools to shift these unconscious beliefs and programs (and any others that arise).

Some of the common programs people clear in our trainings are:

- I'm not good enough
- I can't lose weight
- I can't find a good relationship
- I can't have a successful business
- I can't earn more than $X
- I am unworthy
- I have a fear of rejection
- I am unlovable
- I have a fear of failure
- Nobody can help me
- Life is hard
- I can't be happy.

STUDENT STORY:

Examples: Whilst working with a fellow student in our Master Practitioner training, one of our students, Brendon, was able to clear a huge belief that was holding him back from going to the next level in his career.

At the time he was still working in the construction industry and he very much wanted to take the leap to move into coaching full time and step away from the physical labour job.

The belief he held was that he would be lazy if he didn't have a physical job. This belief stemmed from his father and grandfather both having physical jobs growing up. Working with a fellow student in the training using Time Line Therapy Techniques®, Brendon was able to shift this belief. He subsequently quit working in the construction industry and is now coaching full time (and doesn't feel lazy at all!). He feels 1000x more fulfilled than any project he ever built and is also making the most money he ever has before.

Did you consciously choose all the belief patterns that you hold?

Do you know what beliefs could be creating your life experience right now?

What would happen if you started to explore and clear these beliefs just like Brendon did?

To find out more about our life-changing courses head to evolveandrelaunch.com.au/evolveyourmind and download our interactive free PDF workbook for Evolve Your Mind to complete all these activities plus the guided audios and videos to support this book.

CHAPTER 6

EMOTIONS ARE ENERGY IN MOTION

> *'How you think and how you feel creates your state of being. The quantum field responds to how you are being.'*
> **– Dr Joe Dispenza**

In this fast paced, modern world it is all too easy to live in your thoughts. To live in your mind can cause dissociation from your body and emotions.

As you witness yourself in the moment, become aware of where your energy is focused in this moment. Now draw your attention to your breath. Now draw your awareness to your feet, hands, legs and back and observe how they are feeling. A quick scan like this can highlight the amount of your awareness that is outside of your body.

It can be common for people to perceive their body as an unsafe place to exist if the mind becomes their home. There are a number of reasons for this, but one of the biggest is that, often as children, people have been taught that negative emotions were not okay and so it's common to develop habits of repressing them.

For example, you might have fallen over and started crying and been told *'don't cry'* or *'don't be upset'*. Although well intentioned, this process of repression can become a subconscious protection mechanism that kicks in. When you experience emotions such as anger, sadness, fear, hurt, guilt, to name a few, often the message you received was that they are not acceptable emotions to display, and so you may have learnt to repress them. When it's repressed, that emotion (energy in motion) has to go somewhere and, for most people, the body becomes the storehouse of unexpressed emotions.

Imagine for a moment you are in a swimming pool and you have a beach ball on the surface of the water. This beach ball represents an emotion. When you try to suppress an emotion, it is the equivalent of trying to hold that ball underneath the water.

As you grew up, you may have developed a strategy of repressing several emotions and that energy becomes quite intense. What also happens is, when you least expect it, something triggers you and the repressed emotions pop up just like a beach ball underneath the water. When you have had an argument or have been under the influence of alcohol, all these beach balls (in the form of unresolved emotion) can bubble up and surface.

Over time, this can also add up and accumulate and, like the straw that breaks the camel's back, a very minor incident can result in a large emotional response because of the past repressed emotions that get released when you are triggered.

In the Evolve and Relaunch Education trainings, you learn tools to safely reach underneath the surface, release the valve and allow all the air to come out of the beach balls so you can easily pull the deflated ball of energy up to the surface.

STUDENT STORY:

In 2017, one of our students, Tracey, enrolled in our Perth NLP Practitioner training. She had been a passenger on the Costa Concordia ship which sunk off the coast of Italy in January 2012 and suffered from diagnosed PTSD ever since. She would experience the emotions of panic, fear and anxiety whenever she was confined in small places or dark rooms. She couldn't go shopping, to the movies or concerts, out for dinner, be on a train, buses, boats, and could do nothing involving water (which, as an aqua aerobics instructor, was difficult). She was experiencing about 20-30 panic attacks a day when she attended the training. Tracey had previously attempted to resolve her symptoms by seeing several experts such as psychologists and EMDR experts and had spent tens of thousands of dollars trying to get treatment.

During the Evolve and Relaunch Evolved NLP Practitioner training, Tracey experienced symptoms of panic and anxiety. So, Paul demonstrated helping her to clear her emotions of fear and anxiety using Time Line Therapy® techniques and within 10 min-

utes she felt completely different. Tracey went on to study hypnotherapy and Master Practitioner of NLP with Evolve and Relaunch Education and still credits that experience with Paul as life-changing.

In our courses, you will learn simple processes to work with the unconscious mind to clear these stored emotions easily and effortlessly. Now, this doesn't mean that you will become a robot and never feel these emotions ever again. What it means is that you will start to feel and experience your emotions in the moment (a rational level of the emotion rather than a lifetime of built-up and repressed emotion that comes out when triggered or activated). It allows you to respond instead of react.

Emotions are useful feedback mechanisms for us when they are rational amounts appropriate to our experience of the present moment. Anger allows us to set boundaries and speak up, sadness allows us to feel and experience the contrast to joy, but too much built up emotion that has not been expressed can cause issues not only mentally but physically as well.

It takes a lot of energy for you to repress and suppress stored emotion. So, the releasing process is very therapeutic and we have even had students tell us they feel 10kg lighter after learning how to release the emotional weight they are carrying using these tools.

ACTIVITY:
What are some negative emotions you regularly experience?

_____
_____
_____
_____

Do you feel anger or frustration? Sadness, anxiety or worry? Fear, shame, guilt or doubt? Becoming aware of them is the first step to releasing them.

Extra activity for self-awareness: Consider the last time you felt angry or frustrated. What triggered it? Was it a rational amount of anger or frustration considering the incident?

Bonus challenge: Start to keep a thought and emotion journal. Every night review and log the emotions you experienced during the day and what triggered them. Also start to write down your day-to-day thoughts and take notice of any patterns or themes.

CHAPTER 7

CHANGING YOUR PAST

> *'I am not what happened to me,*
> *I am what I choose to become.'*
> **– Carl Jung**

Everyone has a past. And chances are, your past feels real to you.

Have you ever taken the time to consider where your past actually exists?

If you think about it for a moment, your past only ever exists in one place—in your own mind.

Your past is a recalled cluster of your perspective of experiences which you deleted, distorted and generalised and now you call that 'cluster' of mental memories real.

In fact, your past is more like a photocopy of a photocopy of the experiences you had. They become blurred and misinterpreted the more we recall them.

Have you ever tried to share a memory with a family member, only to have them recall a completely different perspective of the situation?

There are numerous accounts of police reports from crime scenes with witness' accounts differing at the exact same event.

In 1974, psychologist Elizabeth Loftus was interested in understanding how information can affect an eyewitness' account of an event and conducted studies on the impact of leading information in terms of both imagery and differing language in relation to eye witness testimonies.

To test this, Loftus and Palmer asked 45 people to estimate the speed of motor vehicles in 7 films of traffic accidents, ranging in duration from 5 to 30 seconds using different forms of questions.

After watching the accidents, the participants were asked to describe what had happened as if they were eyewitnesses. They were asked various specific questions, including 'About how fast were the cars going when they either smashed, collided, bumped, hit or contacted each other?'

Participants who were asked the "smashed" question thought the cars were going faster than those who were asked the "hit" question.

The participants in the "smashed" condition reported the highest speed estimate (65.6 km/h), followed by "collided" (63.25 km/h), "bumped" (61.32 km/h), "hit" (54.7 km/h), and "contacted" (51.17 km/h) in descending order.

That is almost 15 km difference of perception of the same event simply by the way the question was asked!

Loftus' findings seem to indicate that our memories and perception might be altered simply by the way questions are asked after an event. The original memory can be modified, changed or supplemented.

Changing our perceptions and memories can be useful in certain contexts. In our Evolve and Relaunch Education Practitioner trainings, we teach you tools and techniques to help you change your perception of past memories and events so these memories and events no longer hold you back but instead help you to move forward in life.

ACTIVITY TO EXPLORE YOUR TIMELINE:
Take a deep breath and remember something that happened a week ago. If we were to ask you to remember something that happened a week ago, can you point to the direction of where this memory is stored in relation to your body? Many people point behind them in some direction—straight, left or to the right, sometimes even down.

_____
_____
_____
_____

Now, if you were to think of something that will happen in your future, perhaps next week, can you notice which direction you would point that indicates where your future is stored? Many people point in front of themselves in some direction.

BONUS: Download the guided audio of this process to follow along at www.evolveandrelaunch.com.au/evolveyourmind

This storage mechanism allows you to access the place within your thinking BEFORE certain beliefs were formed or negative emotions were first repressed. And if you access the place within your neurology before a limiting belief was formed, the belief can't be present in the now.

There are three reasons why emotions and beliefs disappear when working with Time Line Therapy® techniques:

1. Reframe
2. Metaphysical illusion
3. Quantum physics

These are concepts you will explore further in our trainings, including how to discover the root cause of the beliefs or stored emotions.

Changing your past

There is much more to learn in order to clear limiting beliefs and emotions, but to give you an experience, bring to mind a limiting belief that may be holding you back in your life.

Here is a list of common beliefs that may help:

- I'm not good enough
- I'm unworthy
- I am unlovable
- I can't trust myself
- I can't trust others
- I can't be successful

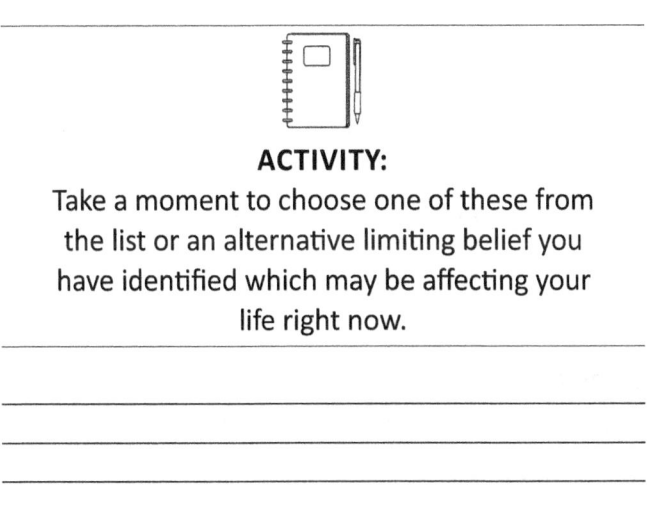

ACTIVITY:
Take a moment to choose one of these from the list or an alternative limiting belief you have identified which may be affecting your life right now.

_____
_____
_____
_____

Now think of a time, an event in your life when you experienced this belief as true.

Now float above that event, all the way before the event looking down on the event and consider what you would have needed to learn in order to let that belief be released. Trust whatever comes to mind, without judgement.

BONUS: Download the guided audio of this process to follow along at www.evolveandrelaunch.com.au/evolveyourmind

For example, if you were to float above and before the event of feeling 'I'm not good enough' from the position of above the event you may be able to learn 'I am unique', 'I can only ever do my best' and 'I am always growing'. These learnings can help to release the negative associations on the event and allow you to feel more resourceful in the present.

In the complete process taught in the training, you will not only learn how to clear the root cause of beliefs such as these but also how to install new beliefs into the timeline directly into your unconscious mind.

Changing your past

STUDENT STORY:

Example:

One of our students, Rachael F, had an incredible experience during her NLP Practitioner training with us. She had previously experienced five miscarriages and, at the age of 44, held a belief that a part of her 'didn't feel good enough to be a mother'.

Juliet demonstrated a powerful technique, a parts integration, in front of the class during the training to help her integrate the conflict and Rachael describes, 'That day was definitely a catalyst to the change in me. I felt electricity inside my stomach and womb afterwards. I felt so different and I remember saying that to a fellow student when we had a tea break in the kitchen. I was due for my period that following week and it just never came. My doctor had finally put me on the right thyroid medication for me, so that may have helped too. It shifted what it needed because here we are with our bub. Luka is our beautiful blessing and I couldn't be happier.'

It's incredibly empowering to understand your life narrative of why certain beliefs have been formed in your life and to be able to finally free yourself of them.

You can also use the power of your timeline to overcome feelings of anxiety in the future.

> *'Anxiety is a warning from your unconscious mind to focus on what you want.'*
> **– Tad James**

It is actually impossible to feel anxious about something that happened in the past. For a moment, consider something in the past that you used to feel anxious about. Where is the anxiety? If you're truly thinking of something from the past it is simply not there.

So by using the mechanics of your internal timeline you can use this to create feelings of certainty in your future. Your chances of success in an outcome are much higher when you feel certain rather than if you are feeling anxious.

These are extremely powerful and empowering tools as once you have learned what you need to, the unconscious mind can let go of the limiting beliefs and stored emotions and free your energy to create what you want in the future.

In our Evolved Hypnotherapy Practitioner training, you also learn how to conduct full hypnotic regressions into your client's past which is extremely powerful for creating change in the present.

ACTIVITY:
Follow the exercise above and practice floating above your future and your past (and any events where you have carried limiting beliefs) and observe how you feel, see and what you notice.

_____
_____
_____
_____

BONUS: Listen to the audio recording for Chapter 7 to be guided through this exercise. PLUS receive a bonus 'Overcoming Anxiety' guided process.

Visit www.evolveandrelaunch.com.au/evolveyourmind to listen.

CHAPTER 8

DESIGN YOUR FUTURE

> *'All you need to do is take one step each day towards your dreams.'*
> **– Juliet Lever**

Your future is not set in stone. And if you carry yesterday's beliefs into today, you're likely to project your past into your future.

When you filter your world through old beliefs you unconsciously repeat the same thoughts and feelings and therefore patterns of action that will draw to you similar challenges or create new versions of identical problems.

In the previous chapter you learnt how you can use your timeline to clear your past emotions and beliefs and also resolve future feelings of anxiety and worry.

In this chapter, you will discover that you can also use your timeline to create your future. What this means is that you can set goals using your timeline so they are effectively implanted in your future into your unconscious mind. This is a technique which is best done with one of our trained NLP practitioners or learnt in a live training with us, so this chapter will cover a few other important points about goal setting.

1. **Goals**
2. **Taking action**
3. **Focus**

***

1. **Goals**

    What are your current feelings about setting goals? For many people, the idea of goal setting is associated with memories or experiences of 'not achieving' things. Often this is because they have tried to set a goal without following the steps explained in the Evolve Manifestation Model in Chapter 2. Because your conscious mind is the goal-setter and your unconscious mind is the goal-getter, you need to ensure that you have alignment of your unconscious mind if you want to achieve a goal. Something that truly helps is forming a clear mental image of your goal to support the unconscious mind in achieving it. **The clearer your mental image is of your desired outcome, the easier the communication will be to your unconscious mind.**

    Another reason people have difficulty achieving their goals is that they set goals that are actually emotional states. For example, 'I just want to be happy' is not a measurable goal. Many of us have heard of SMART goals, but in our courses, you will take this one step further to ensure the mental image of your goal is clear, your feelings and emotions are aligned and the action you take is actually rewarded and it's clear to your unconscious mind.

2. **Taking action**

   When you take action towards anything in life, you want to operate from a psychology AND physiology of excellence. As explained in Chapter 3, the way you feel can impact the way you perceive an event in your life. If you can prime yourself to feel in optimal physiology (your breathing, posture and tonality), you can prime yourself to filter your reality optimally and, if you can clear your filters of perception (beliefs, values, emotions etc), you have a higher chance of filtering for what you want.

   As a result, the action you are going to take is more likely to be rewarded and you can achieve the outcomes you desire, but you must take some sort of action. It is important to create alignment mentally and emotionally before you take action towards your goals.

3. **Focus on what you want**

   One of the most important factors in our training is the constant reinforcement of focusing on what you actually want in life. As mentioned in previous chapters, your unconscious mind does not process negatives. It is very simple and literal and will form mental images that become suggestions to your unconscious mind. So, remember, if someone were to say to you, 'don't think of a fluffy cat on top of a piano', you will actually create a mental unconscious image of it. Your mental images are suggestions to your unconscious mind. So, often people will say things like, 'I just don't want to feel stressed out anymore', which is creating the internal experience of exactly what they don't want. So, start getting in the habit of noticing when you are focusing on what you don't want, and reframe it by asking, 'so what do you want instead'?

Achieving outcomes

NLP was one of the first forms of coaching/therapy to be outcome-based. So, before you start making any changes, you need to first get very clear about precisely what outcome you are trying to achieve.

At this point in the chapter, you may be considering (or already be) studying NLP with us. We invite you to take a moment to get clear on your desired outcome for your life for the future.

ACTIVITY:

What is your desired outcome in an area of your life in the future? Be sure to state it in the way you want it and remember you are the creator of your reality. What will you see, feel, hear when you have this outcome?

_____
_____
_____
_____

STUDENT STORY:

Example: *In our November 2020 NLP Practitioner training, one of our students, Rachael B, decided she wanted to set a goal to quit her job and earn her first $10,000 month in her NLP coaching business within four months. Her previous best income month in business was $3,000.*

Using Time Line Therapy® techniques, we helped her to visualise achieving the goal in sensory-rich detail and then placed it into her future time line. We completed 'certainty checks' so that she felt 100% certain she would achieve her goal.

By March 2021, Rachael was excited to share with her fellow graduates that she had indeed reached over $10,000 income for the month! She also quit her job earlier that year and is now working full time as a mindset coach supporting new business owners to achieve their goals.

CHAPTER 9

KEEP EVOLVING

> *'I want you to get excited about who you are, what you are, what you have, and what can still be for you. I want to inspire you to see that you can go far beyond where you are right now.'*
> **– Virginia Satir**

Now that you have read through all these chapters, you would have a better understanding of what can be unlocked within yourself by learning NLP. NLP is **so much more** than a set of techniques— it is about having an attitude of curiosity and a methodology of modelling ways for you to achieve results in life, and help others too!

It is also a reminder that all change, learning and behaviour is unconscious. So, if you can communicate and make change with your unconscious mind then you are far more likely to create change in your life.

Take a moment now to come back to your intention for reading this book and think about why you want to study NLP. Is it to improve your financial situation? Is it to help others? Is it to have better relationships or health? Or even create greater self-awareness?

Many of our students choose to study with us simply because they are curious and they want more out of life. Many people want to add the skills to their existing business or occupation. Others want to step into a career change and do something completely different and be paid for it.

Regardless of the intention, the concepts taught in our trainings are applicable across contexts and, if you think about it, you are always coaching others and yourself in life. If you have children, you are coaching them every time you try to get them to do something. If you have a team at work, you are coaching them to get results. If you want to get fit, you are coaching yourself to get up and go to the gym when your alarm goes off in the morning. These skills truly level up your self-awareness, your self-confidence and the way you perceive and filter your reality.

In our Master Practitioner of NLP training, we also dive deeper into concepts such as your personal values and deeper unconscious programs as well as shadow work. Shadow work is not traditionally taught in NLP trainings however we have included it because we find it helps our students create deeper alignment and wholeness. The reality is, only when we can learn to accept and integrate all parts of ourselves, that's when true healing can occur.

In our Hypnotherapy Practitioner and Advanced Hypnosis trainings we teach non-script-based hypnotherapy skills to help our students develop deep intuitive hypnosis skills and truly 'go with' their clients to help them achieve lasting results. These skills also carry across to more intuition and confidence in all areas of life including coaching and public speaking.

We have students from all over the world and would love to welcome you to one of our trainings soon. We have done our absolute best to share as much value as we possibly can within the pages of this book, and also trust you can appreciate the power of live transformation will always far outweigh the power of written information.

Therefore; one of the final activities we encourage you to do is to imagine your future making changes and a commitment to yourself today:

ACTIVITY:
Imagine your life in 20 years' time having spent time unlocking your past beliefs, programming and understanding yourself and the world at a deeper level.

Now image your life in 20 years' time carrying those old unresourceful beliefs around in your life.

Which future seems full of more potential?

Which future do you want to choose.... now?

Listen to the audio recording for Chapter 9 to be guided through this exercise. Visit www.evolveandrelaunch.com.au/evolveyourmind to listen.

_____
_____
_____
_____

As our final invitation to you, here is a special offer to you for reading this book. If you mention you read this book to us upon registering for a training, you will receive AUD $100 course credit towards your next course with us (also valid for returning students for one new course).

Please like and follow us on social media at Instagram or Facebook (@evolveandrelaunch) and head to our website at www.evolveandrelaunch.com.au/evolveyourmind to download the free resources to support you reading this book.

You will receive valuable updates and details from us about our upcoming courses and events along the way.

We look forward to continuing to help you evolve your mind and relaunch your life.

Keep Evolving,
Paul and Juliet

Testimonials

'Studying with Evolve and Relaunch has been the BEST life-changing decision.

The way Paul and Juliet teach is like no other. They create a stimulating and engaging learning environment and personally invest themselves in every moment with care for each graduate. If you are ready to learn, grow, be challenged, up-level yourself and see the world as a blank slate where you are 100% the creator of your life, this is without a doubt the thing that will change everything.

I signed up to up-level myself as an individual, and what I received in return was a completely new perspective on the human psyche, why and how people operate and most importantly, how to create long-term intentional change within myself and others.

Four courses later, including Masters of NLP and Time Line Therapy®, studying with these guys was the best decision I have done for my personal and professional development.'

Steph, SA

'Evolve and Relaunch, as the name suggests, truly will evolve you as a person more than your imagination and relaunch your life.

The essence of Evolve and Relaunch is the amazing souls, teachers and mentors, Paul and Juliet.

This power couple amplifies your experience with skills, knowledge, and expertise. They bring their all in their training for their students and will give you more than the training and course material (in the literal sense).

Training is tailored in a way that you will learn, grow, and absorb being present in training. I have completed three trainings with Evolve and Relaunch, and I feel my whole world view and life has changed. I have completed many pieces of training and studies before and have never experienced this magical style or teaching methods before.

I suggest all parents and professionals do the NLP training as it will enhance your quality of life, and its ripple effect will be seen in your kids and work.

I know myself so much better with the deep learnings and understanding I have received throughout the training, and I believe in my extraordinary capabilities.

I am so grateful to Paul and Juliet for offering their training with so much love and taking me into the journey of abundance and possibilities of this cosmos.'

Shavleen, WA

'The personal transformation I have experienced is simply priceless. I gained so much more clarity at a deep soul level, I am more confident, focused, more empowered and energised with new found inspiration. Juliet and Paul are such authentic, grounded people, the training itself is very clear, so informative and at times quite entertaining. One of the many bonuses is they have a fabulous fully trained and supportive crew beside them and the community of participants are all likeminded people that you will have in your life for years to come. I am so very grateful to have graduated and become a certified NLP practitioner. My own clients are going to reap all these beautiful benefits too and I can't wait to share with them. Oh, and I instantly signed up to go on to do my Master Practitioner training because once started, I knew I wanted more … such a no brainer, really! The strongest word that comes to mind is freedom!'

Andie, VIC

'This has been the most amazing journey, expanding my awareness and giving me the tools that are resources to change my life and to help others do the same. Paul and Juliet are the most amazing teachers, sharing their wealth of knowledge whilst supporting you on your own journey. I have met the most wonderful people along the way who I now call friends and I feel completely supported by them all for the next part of my journey. The Evolve & Relaunch courses are the BEST investment that you will make in yourself.'

Brooke, WA

'I cannot thank Paul and Juliet enough for the most empowering and incredible incredible life-changing course. After previously studying with another school I was mind blown by the difference.

Paul and Juliet are the perfect duo to do NLP through, in a no bullshit approach, but in a relatable way—there is the perfect balance of humour, being pushed, softness and so many lightbulb moments that I could not have ever imagined learning in this capacity.

Regardless of your life circumstances, background or even location, everyone was transformed after! In 2019, after studying NLP, I overhauled my entire life and now in 2022 I have done the same thing.

If someone was walking into NLP, my one piece of advice is, strap in—life is about to change!'

Sophie Guidolin, Qld

'Just when you think you know yourself there becomes a new level of knowing, and a new level of respect for doing the work to know more! And whilst NLP is the gateway to knowing thyself, Juliet and Paul take the unique learnings to a whole other level. Their style of delivery goes beyond expectation, they integrate the teachings with passion and ease and you can't help but fall in love with wanting to know more with them. They weave their magic together beautifully. No one teaches this work like they do. I cannot recommend Evolve and Relaunch enough!!'

Kim Morrison, Qld

Take the next step in your Evolution

SCAN HERE
to find out more

References

The Secret of Creating Your Future by Tad James 1989, Advanced Neuro Dynamics

Alan Cohen quote https://www.goodreads.com/author/quotes/19734.Alan_Cohen?page=5#:~:text=%E2%80%9CThere%20is%20no%20such%20thing%20as%20a%20necessary%20evil.%E2%80%9D&text=%E2%80%9CWhen%20your%20intention%20is%20clear%2C%20so%20is%20the%20way.%E2%80%9D

Albert Einstein quote: https://www.brainyquote.com/quotes/albert_einstein_385842#:~:text=Albert%20Einstein%20Quotes&text=We%20can't%20solve%20problems%20by%20using%20the%20same%20kind,used%20when%20we%20created%20them.

Being Human: An Interview with Daniel J. Siegel, MD. 2017, September 15). Psychiatric Times. https://www.psychiatrictimes.com/view/being-human-interview-daniel-j-siegel-md

Bruce Lipton quote: https://thecitesite.com/authors/bruce-lipton/#:~:text=Products%20by%20Bruce%20Lipton,-Get%20price!&text=%E2%80%9CYou%20are%20personally%20responsible%20for,for%20everything%20in-%20your%20life.%E2%80%9D&text=%E2%80%9CYour%20perspective%20is%20always%20limited,you%20will%20transform%20your%20mind.%E2%80%9D

Candace Pert quote: https://www.azquotes.com/author/24367-Candace_Pert

Carl Jung quote: https://www.goalcast.com/15-enlightening-carl-jung-quotes/

Difference Between Conscious and Subconscious Mind. 2016, August 5. Pediaa. https://pediaa.com/difference-between-conscious-and-subconscious-mind/

Definition of the Mind: by Dan Siegel. https://www.psychiatrictimes.com/view/being-human-interview-daniel-j-siegel-md

James, T (1989). The Secret of Creating Your Future. Metamorphous Press, U.S.

Joe Dispenza quote: https://www.icreatedaily.com/dr-joe-dispenza-quotes/

Molecules of Emotion: The Science Behind Mind-Body Medicine, Candace Pert, 1999 Simon & Schuster, First Edition

McLeod, S. A. (2014, January 11). "Loftus and Palmer Experiment (1974)": Simply Psychology. www.simplypsychology.org/loftus-palmer.html

Milton Erickson quote: https://www.azquotes.com/author/22892-Milton_H_Erickson

Pert, C.B. (1999). Molecules of Emotion: The Science Behind Mind Body Medicine: Why You Feel the Way You Feel. Simon & Schuster, First Edition

Richard Bandler quote: https://www.azquotes.com/author/24065-Richard_Bandler Tad James quote: https://artistquoteoftheday.wordpress.com/2011/03/02/anxiety-is-a-warning-sign-from-the-unconscious-mind-to-focus-on-what-you-want/

Keep Evolving

Tony Robbins quote: https://www.tonyrobbins.com/tony-robbins-quotes/inspirational-quotes/

Virginia Satir quote: https://quotes.thefamouspeople.com/virginia-satir-4012.php

About the Authors

Juliet Lever and Paul Eliseo are the co-founders of Evolve and Relaunch Education.

With over 20 years of combined experience in the personal development industry, Paul and Juliet have trained a community of students worldwide in NLP and hypnotherapy. As a couple they are deeply passionate about bringing transformational skills and empowering knowledge to coaches and individuals to deepen their healing, confidence, skills and personal transformations.

Paul and Juliet live in South Australia with their dog Max and cat Sunny and offer their worldwide trainings online.

For more, visit www.evolveandrelaunch.com.au or follow us on Instagram @evolveandrelaunch

Notes

Keep Evolving

Keep Evolving

www.ingramcontent.com/pod-product-compliance
Lightning Source LLC
Chambersburg PA
CBHW071702040426
42446CB00011B/1881